Little Bit

The Sound of Short I

By Peg Ballard and Cynthia Amoroso

I can cook
a little bit.

I can make a home run hit.

5

I can learn to kick.

I can hear a clock go tick.

9

I can wear
a wig.

I can help my sister dig.

I can run
up a hill.

15

I can sit on a window sill.

I can dress
like a king.

I can learn to sing.

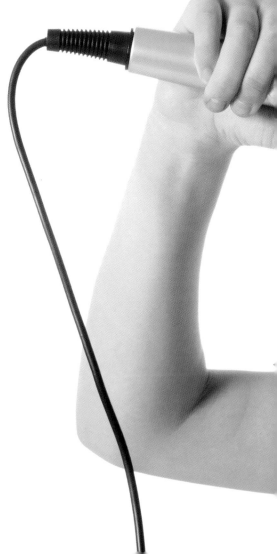

Word List:

bit	sill
dig	sing
hill	sister
hit	sit
kick	tick
king	wig
little	window

Note to Parents and Educators

The books in this series are based on current research, which supports the idea that our brains are pattern-detectors rather than rules-appliers. This means children learn to read easier when they are taught the familiar spelling patterns found in English. As children encounter more complex words, they have greater success in figuring out these words by using the spelling patterns.

Throughout the series, the texts provide the reader with the opportunity to practice and apply knowledge of the sounds in natural language. The books introduce sounds using familiar onsets and *rimes*, or spelling patterns, for reinforcement.

For example, the word *cat* might be used to present the short "a" sound, with the letter *c* being the onset and "_at" being the rime. This approach provides practice and reinforcement of the short "a" sound, as there are many familiar words made with the "_at" rime.

The stories and accompanying photographs in this series are based on time-honored concepts in children's literature: well-written, engaging texts and colorful, high-quality photographs combine to produce books that children want to read again and again.

Dr. Peg Ballard
Minnesota State University, Mankato

The Child's World®
childsworld.com

Published by The Child's World®
1980 Lookout Drive • Mankato, MN 56003-1705
800-599-READ • www.childsworld.com

ACKNOWLEDGMENTS
The Child's World®: Mary Berendes, Publishing Director
The Design Lab: Design
Michael Miller: Editing

PHOTO CREDITS
© BrandX: 9; CEFutcher/iStockphoto.com: 14; Dean
Mitchell/iStockphoto.com: 2; Fertnig/iStockphoto.com: 6;
jwilliams65/iStock.com: 5; Ka2shka/Shutterstock.com: 13;
Lepro/iStockphoto.com: 18; maska82/iStockphoto.com: 10;
Nataliya Turpitko/Shutterstock.com: cover; PeopleImages/
iStockphoto.com: 17; princessdlaf/iStockphoto.com: 20-21

ISBN 9781634070249
LCCN 2015930166

Printed in the United States of America
Mankato, MN
July, 2015
PA02267

ABOUT THE AUTHORS

Dr. Peg Ballard holds a PhD from Purdue University and is an associate professor in the Department of Elementary & Early Childhood Education at Minnesota State University, Mankato. Her areas of expertise are assessment, interventions, and response to intervention. Dr. Ballard teaches online graduate courses in the K-12 reading licensure and master's program along with reading interventions in the undergraduate teacher preparation program.

Cynthia Amoroso holds undergraduate degrees in English and elementary education, and graduate degrees in curriculum and instruction as well as educational administration. She is currently an assistant superintendent in a suburban metropolitan school district. Cynthia's past roles include teacher, assistant principal, district reading coordinator, director of curriculum and instruction, and curriculum consultant. She has extensive experience in reading, literacy, curriculum development, professional development, and continuous improvement processes.